Science 2

for Christian Schools®

BJU PRESS

GREENVILLE, SOUTH CAROLINA

dis·cern·ment

(dĭ-sûrn'mənt)

n. 1. Clear, accurate perception. 2. Sound judgment and keen insight.

The fact that your student has this BJU Press product is evidence that you have exercised not only discernment in your choice of the finest state-of-the-art materials available, but you have also exercised trust—something we remember here every single day. You will not regret choosing a BJU Press Science textbook.

- **Enjoy** interacting with your student to discover the amazing secrets of God's world through daily activities that go beyond reading and include doing.

- **Relax** at test time— your student will be ready and the test prepared for you.

- **Watch** the subject take hold of your student as the process of learning for life begins.

Science 2

for Christian Schools®

Candace J. Levesque
with Dawn L. Watkins

Second Edition

This textbook was written by members of the faculty and staff of Bob Jones University. Standing for the "old-time religion" and the absolute authority of the Bible since 1927, Bob Jones University is the world's leading Fundamentalist Christian university. The staff of the University is devoted to educating Christian men and women to be servants of Jesus Christ in all walks of life.

Providing unparalleled academic excellence, Bob Jones University prepares its students through its offering of over one hundred majors, while its fervent spiritual emphasis prepares their minds and hearts for service and devotion to the Lord Jesus Christ.

> If you would like more information about the spiritual and academic opportunities available at Bob Jones University, please call
> **1-800-BJ-AND-ME** (1-800-252-6363).
> www.bju.edu

NOTE: The fact that materials produced by other publishers may be referred to in this volume does not constitute an endorsement by BJU Press of the content or theological position of materials produced by such publishers. The position of BJU Press, and of Bob Jones University, is well known. Any references and ancillary materials are listed as an aid to the student or the teacher and in an attempt to maintain the accepted academic standards of the publishing industry.

SCIENCE 2 for Christian Schools®
Second Edition

Candace J. Levesque
Dawn L. Watkins

Design	**Composition**	**Project Coordinator**
John Bjerk	Kelley Moore	Vic Ludlum
Elly Kalagayan		
Wendy Searles		

Produced in cooperation with the Bob Jones University Department of Science Education of the School of Education, the College of Arts and Science, and Bob Jones Elementary School.

Special acknowledgement is given to Emil Silvestru from Answers in Genesis (esilvestru@answersingenesis.org) for his help on pp. 22-23 (fossil map).

Photo credits appear on pages 182-83.

for Christian Schools is a registered trademark of BJU Press.

© 1989, 1998, 2003 BJU Press
Greenville, South Carolina 29614
First Edition © 1975 BJU Press

Printed in the United States of America
All rights reserved

ISBN 1-57924-911-6

15 14 13 12 11 10 9 8 7 6 5 4 3 2 1

Contents

1 How Long Do Plants Live? — 1

2 The History of the Earth — 13

3 Forces — 29

4 Your Bones — 43

5 A Round Earth — 55

6 Light and Shadows — 67

7 Living and Not Living — 79

8 How Long Is It? — 93

9 How Earth Moves — 105

10 Your Muscles — 115

11 Layers of the Earth — 125

12 Where Things Live — 135

13 Motion — 149

14 Ocean Shorelines — 161

Little Things Count — 172

Useful Terms — 174

Index — 181

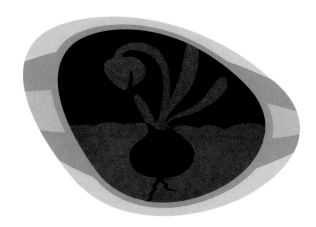

How Long Do Plants Live?

CHAPTER ONE

*"And the Lord God planted a garden eastward in Eden;
and there he put the man whom he had formed."*

Genesis 2:8

Gardeners are people who plan, plant, and care for
flower beds and gardens. To do those jobs, gardeners
have to know many things. One thing they have to know
is that plants can be sorted into groups by how long the
plants live.

*"The grass withereth, the flower fadeth: but the word of
our God shall stand for ever."*   *Isaiah 40:8*

When plants are sorted into groups by how long they live, there are three groups. One group has plants that live only one year. Another group has plants that live two years. The third group has plants that live many years.

Think about the plants in your yard. Can you think of any plants that live year after year? Did you think of trees? Maybe you didn't know that trees are plants. They are, and they live a long time. Some live for a hundred years or more. Many bushes and shrubs live for years too. Do you have any plants that live only one year? If you have a vegetable garden, you have many plants that live only one year. You may even have a few plants that live two years. Carrots, beets, and turnips can live two years if you don't pick and eat them the first year.

Planning a Garden

A garden is a plot of land for growing plants, and a flower bed is a special plot just for flowers. A site is the whole area around a building. It is the front yard, the back yard, and the side yards. Before a gardener starts planting anything, he should know how his whole site is to look in the end. Read this talk between a gardener and the person planning the site.

Planner: Why don't you look at other sites to get ideas?

Gardener: What do I look for?

Planner: Well, first you might look for how the earth, rocks, water, and plants are used. Then you could look for things people have added. Here's a list of some of those things.

1. greenhouses, toolsheds, and playhouses

2. seats, tables, barbecues, and umbrellas

3. statues, fountains, birdbaths, and wells

4. gazebos and pavilions

5. walks, roads, and decks

6. walls and fences

7. steps and bridges

Planner: Now, here is a site plan of the White House in our nation's capital. Notice how many things from the list were used on the site plan of the White House.

walkway

seat   seat

pavilion   The East Garden   birdbath/pool

walkway

road

fountain

Gardener: OK, I've got some ideas from the list. What do I do next?

Planner: Just answer some questions. Do you need a children's play area or an outdoor cooking area?

Gardener: Yes, I'd like both.

Planner: Do you want a flower bed?

Gardener: Oh, yes. I want at least two flower beds by the front door.

Planner: I'll add those to the site plan and get back to you in a week or so. For now, here is an example of a site plan. It will give you an idea of how your plan will look.

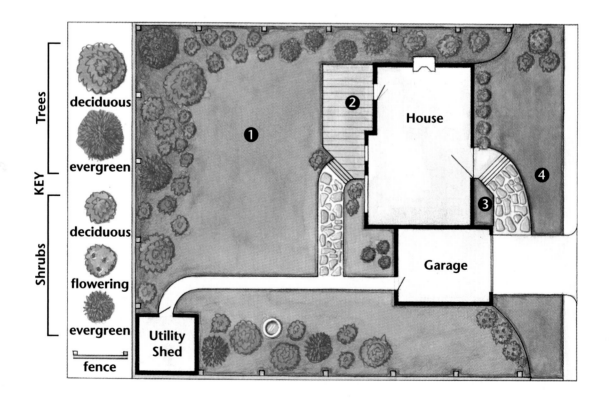

Gardener: Is there anything else we need to do?

Planner: After I add the flower beds to the site plan, we can decide what building materials we need. Then while I go to work putting this plan into action, you can choose what flowers you will use.

After the site is planned, a gardener chooses plants to use. To make good choices, he needs to know how long the plants live. In some gardens he puts plants that live many years next to plants that live just one year. In other gardens he puts only plants that live one year. Study the pictures of different kinds of flower gardens.

Planting a Garden

Gardeners have several ways to find out how long plants live. They can get this information from a seed package or from a nursery. Did you know that there is more than one kind of nursery? You probably know the kind where babies are cared for. Another kind grows and sells small plants. Have you ever visited a plant nursery? What did you see? Look at the picture of the front of a seed package and the picture of the back of a seed package. What can you find out?

Purple Coneflower $1.19

NET WT 2 g

Purple Coneflower
Sow early spring—blooms midsummer to fall

Purple Coneflower. Perennial. Long-lived plants produce beautiful, long lasting, 4-inch purple flowers, each with a striking, bronze, cone-shaped center that attracts butterflies and bees. Ht. 2 to 3 ft.

PREPARATION
Select a sunny location. Loosen well-drained soil with rake or hoe.

PLANT
For easier planting, mix seeds with a cup of sand or vermiculite and spread over the garden area. Lightly rake seed into soil and cover with 1/8 in. of soil, peat moss, or fine sand. Keep moist until seeds germinate in 15-20 days.

TIPS
Drought-resistant plants prefer dry soil and need little watering. For additional plants, divide established clumps in spring or fall.

Finding Out...

About Planting Seeds

1. Get

a package of flower seeds

2. Read the steps for planting the seeds.

3. Find out what time of year the seeds should be planted.

4. Choose a place to plant the seeds. Do they need a special place? How much light will the plant need when it grows? What soil is best?

5. Make the soil ready the way the seed package says.

6. Plant the seeds.

Caring for a Garden

To care for his garden, a gardener needs to know how long plants live. Here is a monthly plan for taking care of plants that live year after year.

JANUARY

Read the gardening notes from last year. Order any new plants or seeds that you want. Check your winter mulch.

Mulch comes from a word that means "soft." It is any material that gardeners put on the ground around plants to keep the roots safe and to keep weeds from growing up too near. Gardeners sometimes use straw or sawdust as mulch. Can you think of anything else gardeners might use?

FEBRUARY

Trim leafless shrubs. Look for roots that have come out of the soil. Carefully press them back into the soil. Add more mulch to those plants. Sharpen your tools. Take notes.

What are some tools gardeners use? Rakes, spades, hoes, and clippers? Which would get dull? How would they get dull? Why is it important to take care of tools?

The gardener writes down which plants grew best in each bed. He might also record how fast they grew and how much water they needed. What notes do you think this gardener made about the roots that came out of the soil?

MARCH

As the weather warms up, remove the mulch from plants that are beginning to grow. After the ground thaws, fertilize the plants. Transplant any plants that need transplanting. Soon the seeds and plants that you ordered will start to arrive. Mark each seed package with the date that the seeds are to be planted. Check the plants for damage and disease. Store the plants in a damp and cool place until you plant them. Take notes.

APRIL

Remove all leftover mulch. Begin to stake plants. Watch for insects and disease. Take notes.

A stake is a stick or a pole that stands beside a plant. The plant is tied to it with soft strips of cloth. Why would some plants need to be tied up this way?

MAY

Plant your seeds. Stake plants as needed. Take notes.

JUNE

Enjoy your garden! Remove dead flowers. Transplant the plants that you ordered. Take notes.

JULY

Water and weed your plants. Use mulch to help keep in moisture and cut down on weeds. Take notes.

AUGUST

Cut back the plants that have finished blooming, but keep some leaves. Order the fall and spring flowering bulbs, such as tulips. Take notes.

SEPTEMBER

Prepare flower garden for fall planting. Take notes.

OCTOBER

Clean up garden. Remove stakes. Tie them in a bundle. Take notes.

NOVEMBER

Gather materials for winter mulching. Mulch the plants when the ground has frozen. Clean and store tools. Take notes.

DECEMBER

Rest! Most of the work is finished. Think about next year. Get your notes together.

The History of the Earth

It is easy to understand how scientists study things that they can see or watch. They call watching "observing." But scientists did not observe the earth's history. So how do they study it? Scientists study the rocks for clues to what happened to the earth in the past.

Ideas About the Beginning

There are two main ideas, or beliefs, about how the earth was made. One idea is called *creation*. The other is called *evolution*.

People who believe the Creation theory believe that God made the earth. They also believe that God changed the earth at least two times in the past. The Bible says that the earth changed when God cursed it and when God destroyed it with a flood. People who believe the evolution theory believe that the earth made itself. They also believe that the earth changed many times in the past. Each theory has a different way to explain the clues scientists find in the rocks.

Fossil Clues

There are many clues to help scientists guess what happened in the earth's history. Perhaps the most important clues come from fossils.

Fossils are parts of living things and marks made by living things that are preserved by nature. Study the pictures. Which things are fossils? Why do you say so?

How Do Fossils Form?

Clue 1: **Things buried quickly can become fossils.**

Clue 2: **Fossils are found nearly everywhere.**

Clue 3: **Many fossils are found in groups.**

Fossils can form when parts of living things or marks made by living things get trapped quickly by mud or sand. Most often a flood moves enough mud fast enough to bury living things. Many kinds of fossils are formed that way.

Clue 1: **Things buried quickly can become fossils.**

Things that have turned to rock are petrified things. These petrified things are kinds of fossils. Tracks preserved in rocks are also kinds of fossils. Find the pictures of petrified things.

Sometimes mud hardens around a living thing. Then the living thing rots and leaves a hole in the rock. This hole is called a mold.

Molds of very thin things like leaves are called imprints.

If a mold later fills with mud that hardens, a cast of the living thing forms. Molds, imprints, and casts are kinds of fossils.

Sometimes all that is preserved of a plant or animal is a black outline on the rock. This black copy is left by carbon, an important material found in all living things. A carbon copy is a kind of fossil.

19

Do you see something on this page that looks like a hairy elephant? It is an animal from long ago called a "woolly mammoth." Is that a good name for it? What would you have named it? Scientists have found woolly mammoths frozen in the ground and stuck in tar pits. These kinds of fossils look much like the living things that they once were.

Amber is also a kind of fossil. Amber is tree sap that is preserved. Sometimes insects and leaves were trapped in the tree sap before it was preserved.

Look at the picture of the amber. Do you see the insect?

About Molds, Imprints, and Casts

1. Get

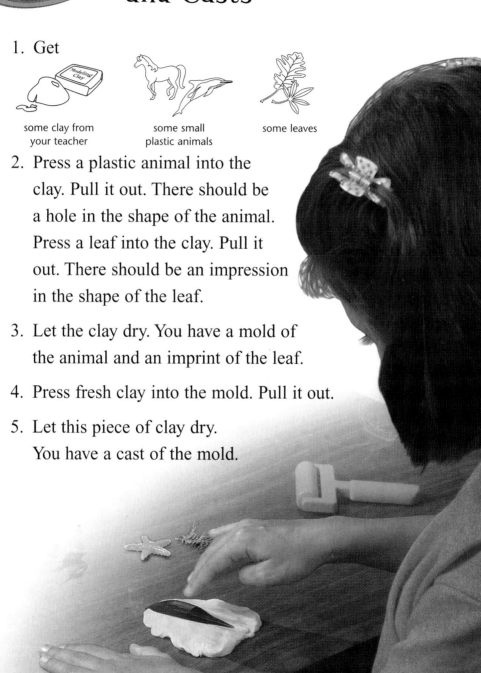

some clay from
your teacher

some small
plastic animals

some leaves

2. Press a plastic animal into the
   clay. Pull it out. There should be
   a hole in the shape of the animal.
   Press a leaf into the clay. Pull it
   out. There should be an impression
   in the shape of the leaf.

3. Let the clay dry. You have a mold of
   the animal and an imprint of the leaf.

4. Press fresh clay into the mold. Pull it out.

5. Let this piece of clay dry.
   You have a cast of the mold.

Where Are Fossils Found?

Most fossils are found in rocks that formed when muddy water settled and dried up. Where are such rocks found? Look at the map. Are those rocks found in many places? Would you find fossils in many places?

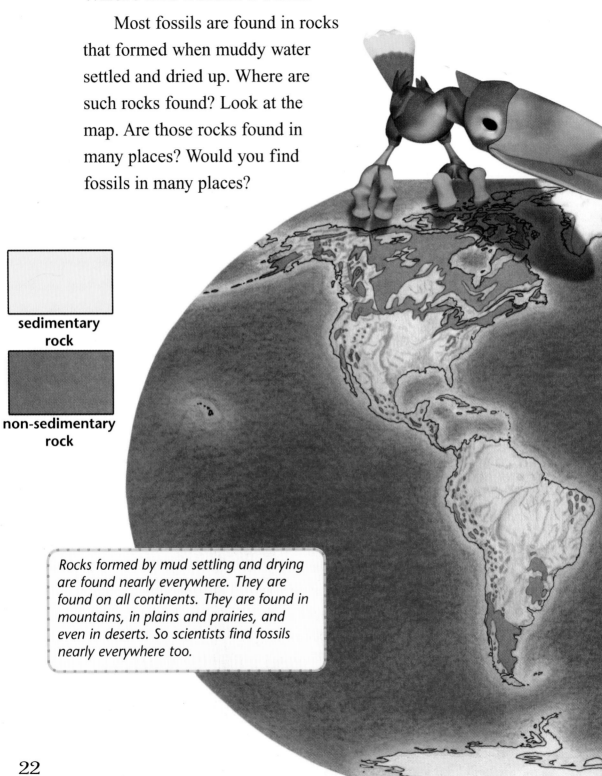

sedimentary rock

non-sedimentary rock

Rocks formed by mud settling and drying are found nearly everywhere. They are found on all continents. They are found in mountains, in plains and prairies, and even in deserts. So scientists find fossils nearly everywhere too.

Clue 2: **Fossils are found nearly everywhere.**

Many Creationists believe that the worldwide Flood in Noah's time made most of the water-formed rocks in about a year.

Many evolutionists believe that many oceans, lakes, and small floods made most of the water-formed rocks over millions and millions of years.

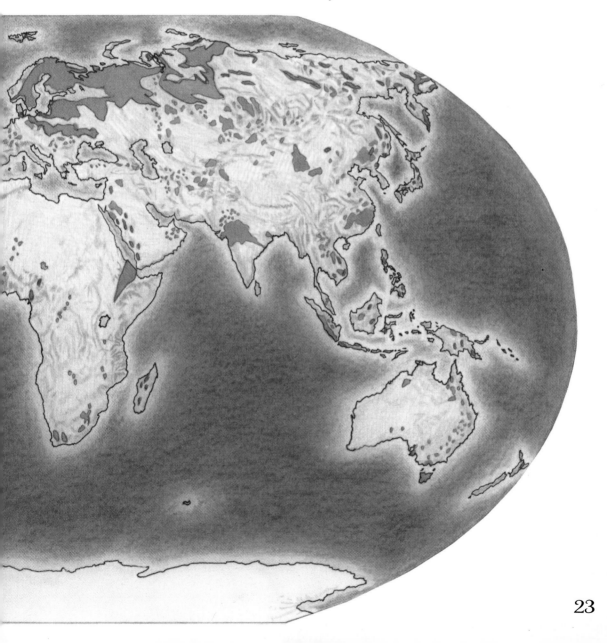

23

About Fossils

1. If you live in a place where there are rocks formed from water, take a walk with your teacher or parents. Look for some rocks that seem to be made of layers of hard mud or sand. If you live in a place where there are no rocks formed from water, get some magazines to find some pictures of such rocks.

2. Look for places on your walk, or in your pictures, where the ground has been worn down or dug into. Look for places where workmen have blasted the ground to build roads or railroad beds. Look for places where water has made gullies. Look along streambeds.

3. On your walk, you may want to look for fossils when you find rocks formed from water. If you find any fossils, call a nearby museum or college to report your find.

Fossils in Groups

Many fossils are found in groups. There are about a dozen main groups in all. One group of fossils has sponges, snails, jellyfish, and crablike creatures called trilobites. Another group has sharks, lungfish, frogs, and land plants. A third fossil group has ducks, pelicans, and dinosaurs.

Clue 3: **Many fossils are found in groups.**

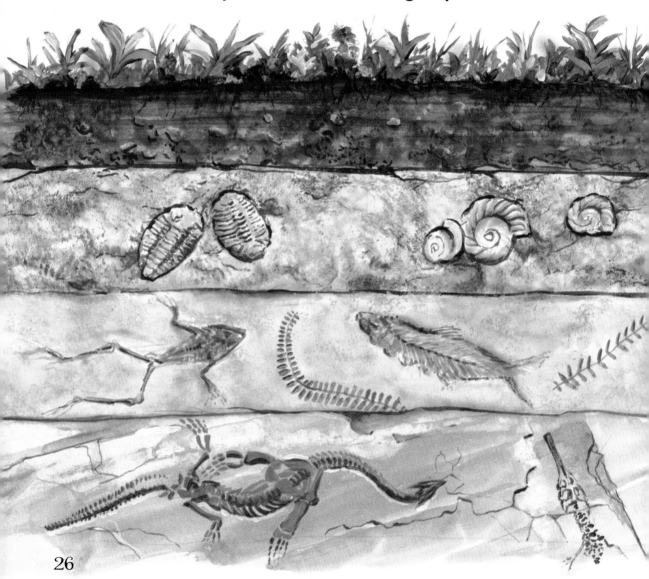

Many Creationists believe that each group once lived in a different area. Many evolutionists believe that each group once lived in a different time.

Creationists say that their theory explains the clues the best. Evolutionists say that their theory explains the clues the best.

The main question should be, Do you believe the Bible to be God's Word? If you do, then the Creation theory is the only theory to explain the clues. If you do not believe the Bible to be God's Word, see what the Bible says about people who are *willingly ignorant* about such things as the history of the earth.

"There shall come in the last days scoffers, . . . saying, Where is the promise of his coming? for since the fathers fell asleep, all things continue as they were from the beginning of the creation.

"For this they willingly are ignorant of, that by the word of God the heavens were of old, and the earth standing out of the water and in the water:

"Whereby the world that then was, being overflowed with water, perished." II Peter 3:3-6

3

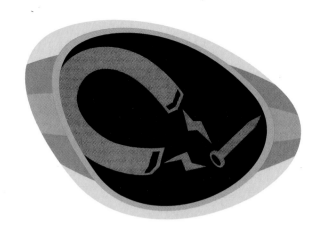

Forces

A push or a pull is a force. When you shove your chair under your desk, you use a push. When you drag a sled up a hill, you use a pull. There are pushes and pulls at work all the time everywhere. God made forces that work in our world.

Gravity

The earth and moon cause a force. Your desk and book cause a force. Even your pencil causes a force! That force is gravity. All objects cause a force called gravity.

Gravity makes many things come down. The earth's gravity pulls many things down to the earth. The moon's gravity pulls many things to the moon. Big objects cause enough gravity to pull other things. Big objects cause more gravity than small things. Your book and desk cause gravity. But do they cause enough to pull things to them? Why not?

Look at the pictures. What objects are coming down?

Gravity makes objects have weight. The earth's gravity makes things have weight. The moon's gravity makes things have weight. Weight is how much of a pull gravity has on something. If something is big, gravity has a big pull on it. People say that the object is heavy. If something is small, gravity has a small pull on it. People say that the object is light. People use a scale to find out how much pull gravity has on things.

Look at the scale in each picture. How much pull does gravity have on each object?

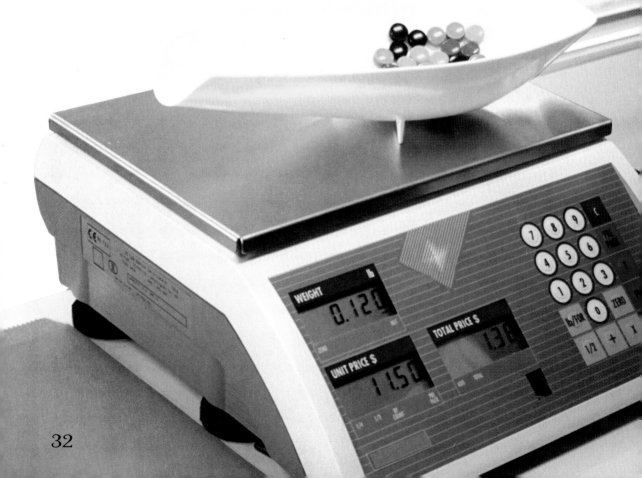

Magnetic Force

Magnets cause a force called magnetic force. Magnetic force makes certain objects come toward the magnet. Magnetic force *attracts* objects made of the metals iron, nickel, and cobalt. Magnets also attract things made partly of those metals.

Magnetic force is stronger in some areas of a magnet than in other areas. Magnetic force is stronger in the ends of a bar magnet than in the middle. Magnetic force is stronger in the ends of a horseshoe magnet than in the middle. The areas of stronger magnetic force are called the poles of the magnet. Look at the picture of a bar magnet. The poles are marked with the letters *N* and *S* because magnet poles are called north and south poles.

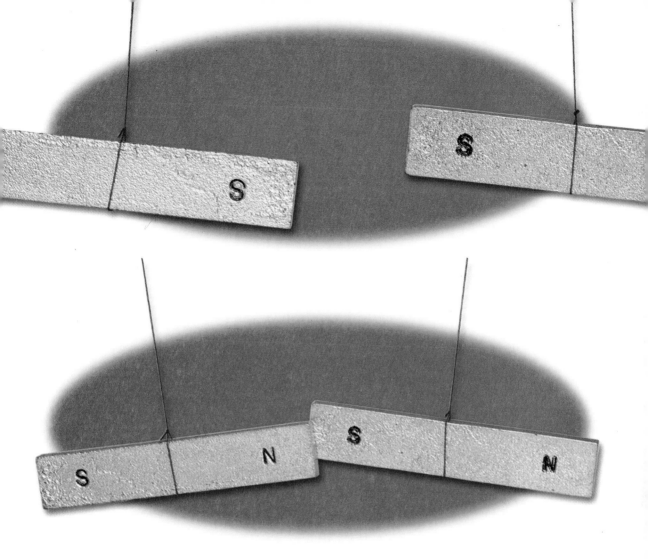

Study the pictures. What happens when the south pole of one magnet is next to the south pole of another magnet? What happens when the north pole of one magnet is next to the south pole of another magnet?

When the south pole of one magnet is next to the south pole of another magnet, the poles push away from each other. These poles repel. *When the north pole of one magnet is next to the south pole of another magnet, the poles* attract.

1. Put

an eraser   a plastic button   a penny

some staples   a nail   a metal paper clip

into

a paper bag

2. Place a magnet inside the paper bag and shake the bag.

3. Guess what will stick to the magnet. Record your guesses in the notebook.

4. Take out the magnet and see what is sticking to it.

5. Record what you see.

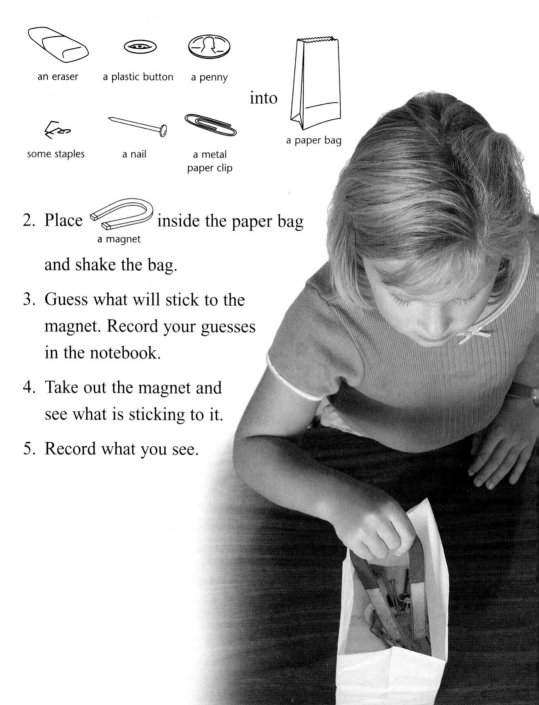

36

Mechanical Force

Sometimes force changes how things move. That force is called mechanical force.

Mechanical force starts movement. It also stops movement. It can make moving things slow down or speed up. It can make them go in another direction. Name the things that are being moved by mechanical force.

"And Moses stretched out his hand over the sea; and the Lord caused the sea to go back by a strong east wind all that night, and made the sea dry land, and the waters were divided."
Exodus 14:21

How is mechanical force
important here?

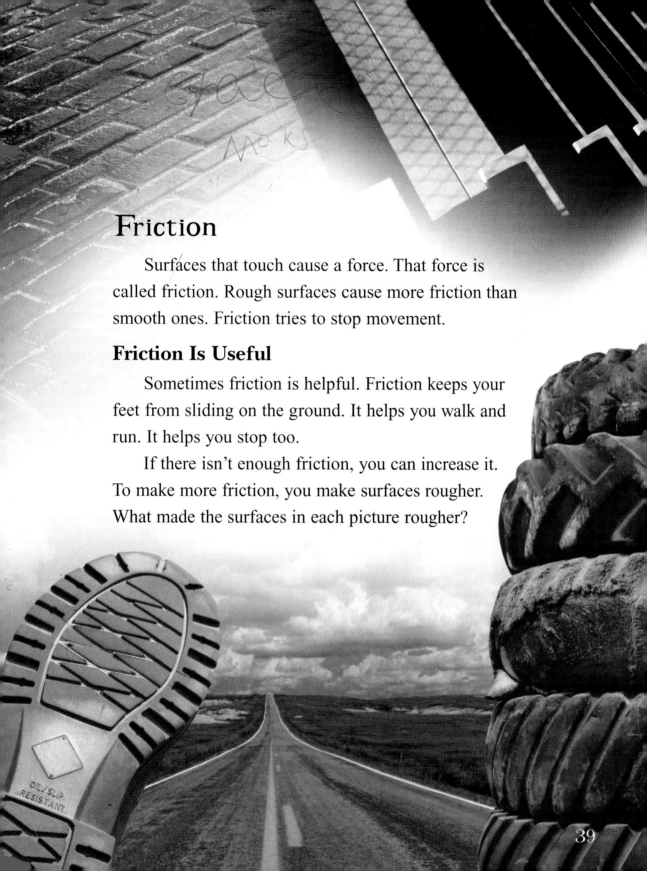

Friction

Surfaces that touch cause a force. That force is called friction. Rough surfaces cause more friction than smooth ones. Friction tries to stop movement.

Friction Is Useful

Sometimes friction is helpful. Friction keeps your feet from sliding on the ground. It helps you walk and run. It helps you stop too.

If there isn't enough friction, you can increase it. To make more friction, you make surfaces rougher. What made the surfaces in each picture rougher?

Friction Can Be a Problem

Sometimes friction is not helpful. Friction makes things like socks or shoelaces wear out. It makes windows or drawers get stuck. It makes wheels squeak and hinges creak. If there is too much friction, sometimes you can make less. To make less friction, you make surfaces smoother. What surface is the boy in the picture making smoother? How is he making it smoother?

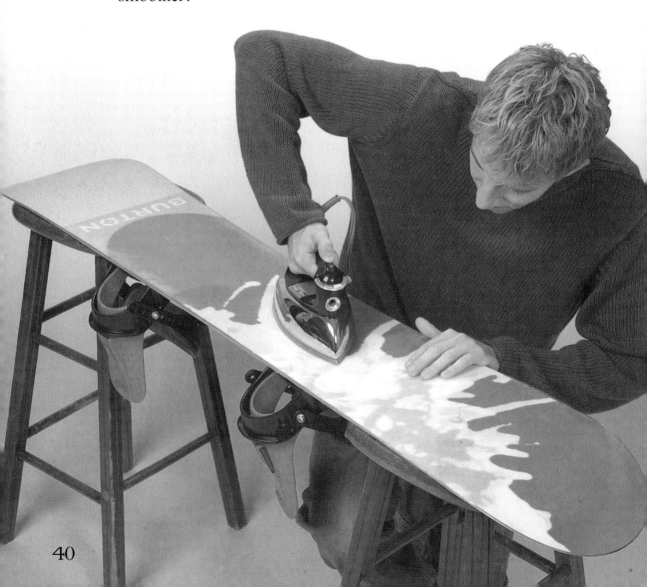

40

There are three kinds of friction. Sliding friction results when two surfaces slide across each other.

Rolling friction happens when something rolls across a surface.

Flowing friction happens between two moving liquids or gases. Or, flowing friction happens between a moving liquid or gas and a solid. Find pictures of each kind of friction.

Finding Out...

About Flowing Friction

1. Get

two tall, clear glasses   some water   some corn syrup   two marbles   a stopwatch or a watch with a second hand

2. Fill one glass with water and the other with corn syrup. Make a label for each glass.

3. Hold a marble against the surface of the water. Let the marble drop. Use the watch to find out how long it takes for the marble to reach the bottom of the glass.

4. Record how long it took.

5. Repeat steps 3 and 4 for the glass of corn syrup.

6. Compare results.

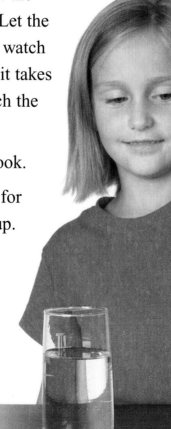

4

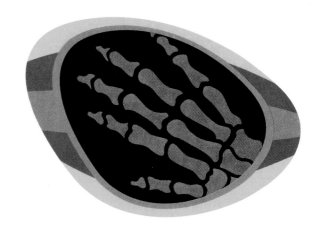

Your Bones

A form as big as your body needs support. God could have given you a shell on the outside. Lobsters have shells. Instead, God gave you a skeleton on the inside.

Parts of the Skeleton

Your skeleton is made of bones and cartilage. Cartilage is a strong, white material. Cartilage bends. Wiggle the end of your nose with a finger and thumb. That part of your nose is cartilage. Feel the top of your ear with a finger and thumb. That part of your ear is cartilage. Cartilage is also found where two or more bones meet.

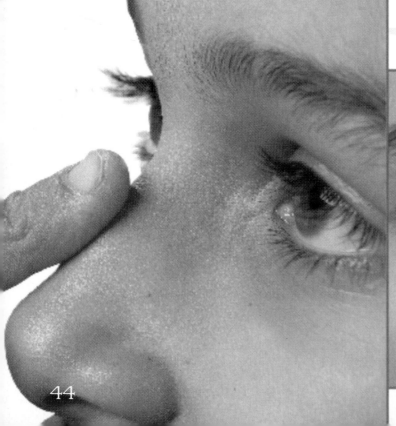

Much of bone is made of minerals, a special kind of matter. Minerals make bones hard. Do you think cartilage has these minerals? Use your finger and thumb and try to wiggle your nose where it meets your forehead. It won't bend because that part of your nose is bone.

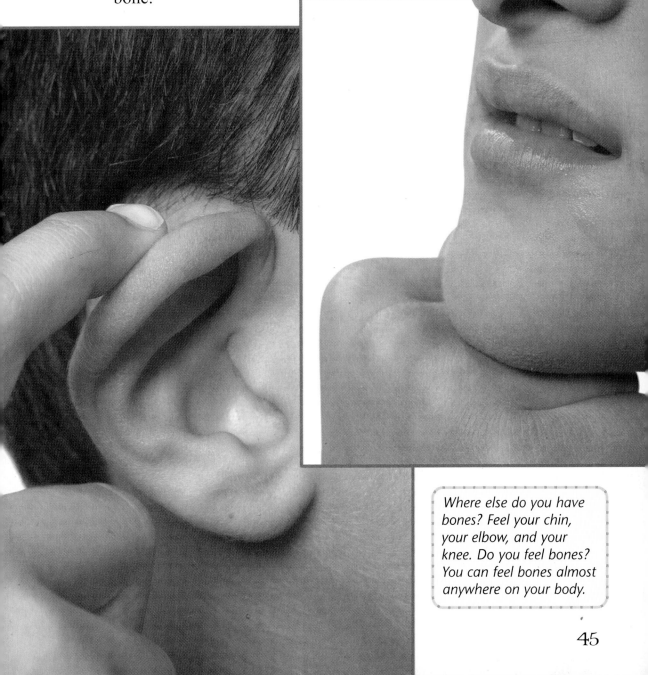

Where else do you have bones? Feel your chin, your elbow, and your knee. Do you feel bones? You can feel bones almost anywhere on your body.

45

Finding Out... About Bones

1. Get

two jars   a rubber glove   a chicken bone   ³/₄ cup of vinegar

three tablespoons of salt   ¹/₂ cup of water   one tablespoon of baking soda

2. Examine the bone. Does it bend?

3. Put the first jar in a place where it won't get knocked over. Watch as your teacher shows you how to mix the vinegar and salt in the jar.

4. Place the bone in the jar with the vinegar and salt.

5. Wait several days; then dissolve one tablespoon of baking soda in ¹/₂ cup of water in the second jar.

6. Wear a rubber glove to remove the bone from the vinegar and salt.

7. Rinse the bone in the baking soda and water solution. Examine the bone again. Does it bend now? What do you think the soaking took out of the bone?

Names of Bones

Study the drawing of the skeleton. How many bone names do you know?

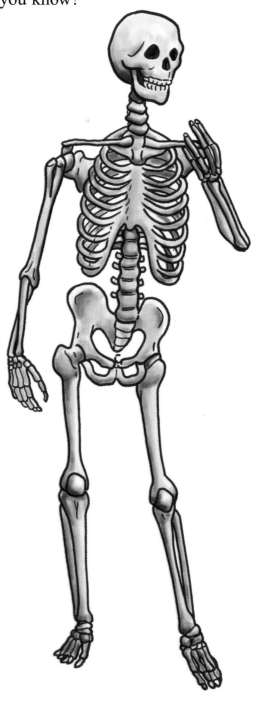

Shapes of Bones

Your bones can be put into groups by shape. You have long bones that are skinny tubes with swollen ends. You have short bones that are wide and chunky. You have flat bones. And you have irregular bones. They are bones that do not fit into any other group. Find pictures of each bone shape.

Your leg, arm, finger, and toe bones are long bones. Your wrist and foot bones are short bones. Your ribs, shoulder, and skull bones are flat bones. And your spine and ear bones are irregular bones.

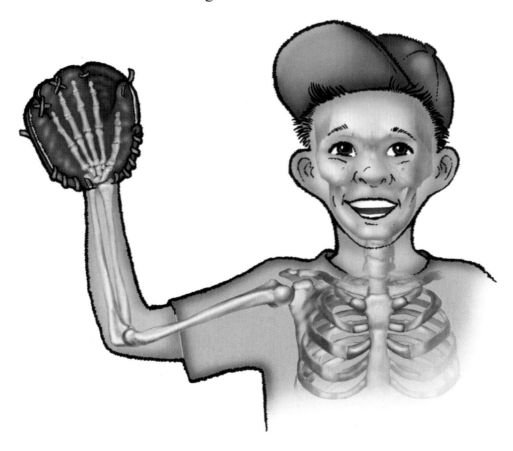

Finding Out...

About Bone Names and Shapes

1. Get

a chicken skeleton

2. Sort the bones into groups by shape. How many long bones did you find? How many flat bones? Can you name any of the bones?

Here is how a chicken skeleton looks. What bones do you see here that are not among the bones you are sorting?

49

Where Bones Meet

The place where two or more bones meet is called a joint. Most joints allow movement. Look at the drawings of some movements. Look at the drawings of some joints. Which allows movement back and forth? Which allows movement up and down?

Your elbow is a hinge joint. It allows up and down movement. Your neck is a pivot joint. It lets your head move back and forth. And your shoulder is a ball-and-socket joint. Hold your arm straight out from your shoulder. Make a big circle with your arm. How do you think a ball-and-socket joint lets bones move?

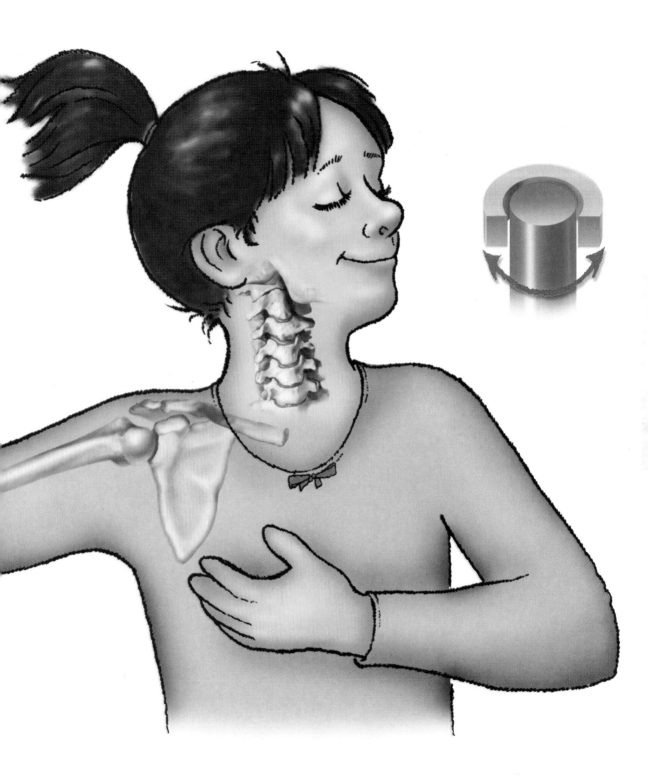

Jobs of the Skeleton

*"Thou hast clothed me with
skin and flesh, and hast fenced
me with bones and sinews."*
Job 10:11

The skeleton has many
jobs. Here are some pictures of
the jobs that the skeleton does.
Which picture shows the skeleton
giving the body shape and support?
Which picture shows the skeleton helping
the body move? Which picture shows the
skeleton protecting the body?

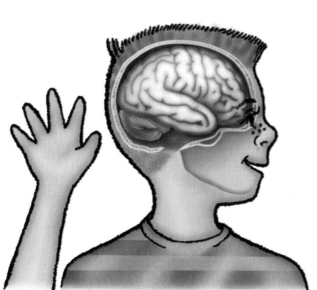

Your leg bones give shape to your legs and support your body.

Your arm and hand bones let you move to play instruments and sports. Your skull protects your brain. Your ribs protect your heart and lungs.

"I will praise thee; for I am fearfully and wonderfully made: marvellous are thy works; and that my soul knoweth right well." *Psalm 139:14*

A Round
Earth

What Is Earth's Shape?

Scientists say that the earth is round. Astronauts see a round earth when they travel in space. But most people see a flat earth. How can this be?

Most people see a flat earth because they see only a small part of it. But astronauts see a round earth because they see the whole thing.

What is round? A plate is round, and a ball is round. But is a plate round like a ball? How are a plate and a ball different? How are they alike?

The earth is round. But is it round like a plate or round like a ball? A model of the earth gives the answer.

A globe is a model of the earth. Is a globe round like a plate or round like a ball? Is the earth round like a plate or round like a ball?

A globe is round like a ball. The earth is round like a ball.

Where Do People Live?

Before people could see pictures of how the earth looks from space, they tried to guess what shape it is. Most people thought that the earth is like a plate. Now people know that the earth is like a ball. They have different ideas about where they live on that ball.

Some people think that they live on flat land on the middle of the earth. Some people think that they live on a flat place at the top of the earth. Some people think that people live in different places all around the earth. Look at the drawings of those ideas. Where do you think people live on the round earth? Why do you say that?

People live in different places all around the earth. Look at the people from the Philippines, Serbia, Nigeria, and Turkey. Do they all speak the same language? Do they look the same? Do they need to know Jesus? How will they hear? Missionaries will take them the gospel.

"Go ye into all the world, and preach the gospel to every creature." Mark 16:15

Finding Out...

About Where People Live

1. Get

your marker strip

some tape

2. Put your marker together.

the globe

3. Find your place on

4. Stick your marker on that place.

5. Tell about where your marker is.

6. Trace a path from your marker to the home marker.

7. Try to trace a different path between those two markers.

What Is Down?

A girl in Australia throws a ball up into the air. The ball comes back down to her, and she catches it. A girl in China throws a ball up into the air. The ball comes back down to her, and she catches it. A boy in Greenland throws a ball up into the air. The ball comes back down to him, but he does not catch it. It falls down to the earth.

No matter where you are on the earth, when you throw things into the air, they come back down to you. All things come back down to the earth.

Look at the figures on the globe. Pretend that they are children from Canada, Mexico, and Poland. Pretend that the dotted lines are the paths their balls take up into the air. Trace the path of each ball with your finger. Did any of the balls fall off the earth? Do any balls ever fall off the earth?

Balls always fall back to the earth. Do you remember why? The earth's gravity pulls them back to the earth. When you throw things up into the air, they come back down to you, no matter where you are on the earth.

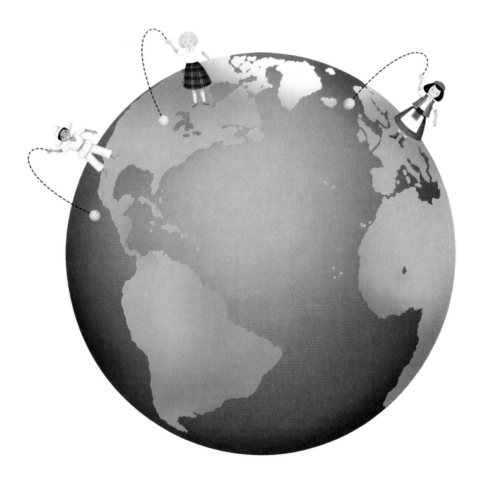

Look at the comic strip. What will happen to the shovels?

The shovels will fall down to the center of the earth. When things are dropped into the ground, they fall toward the center of the earth.

WHAT WILL HAPPEN TO THE GIFTS THEY DROP INTO THE TUNNEL? WILL THEY REACH THE OTHER SIDE?

What do the arrows mean in this picture of the earth? What do things fall toward no matter where they drop from?

"Have ye not known? have ye not heard? hath it not been told you from the beginning? have ye not understood from the foundations of the earth?
"It is he that sitteth upon the circle of the earth, and the inhabitants thereof are as grasshoppers; that stretcheth out the heavens as a curtain, and spreadeth them out as a tent to dwell in."   Isaiah 40:21-22

Light and Shadows

CHAPTER SIX

Light

If you are in the dark, you turn on a light so you can see. Light helps you see. But did you know that there is light that you cannot see?

When you glance at the sun, you can see sunlight at its source. Then that light must travel to Earth to help us see. Between the sun and Earth, light travels in waves we do not see. These waves we call *light energy*.

Where Does Light Come From?

"And God said, Let there be light: and there was light."
Genesis 1:3

God made light, and God made some things that give off light. Man has made some things that give off light too. Look at the pictures. Name the things God made. Name the things man has made.

How are all things that give off light alike?

All things that give off light glow. Can you think of other glowing objects that give off light?

What Does Light Do?

Could you see if your classroom were completely dark? Why? There has to be light for you to see. Light bounces from things to your eyes. Look at the drawing. What things does light let the boy see? What else does light do?

Light not only lets you see, but it also keeps you warm. Have you ever been in the sunshine with your eyes closed? When a cloud passed in front of the sun, did you know without looking that the light was not as strong? How did you know?

Light also helps green plants make food. The energy from the sun helps the plants make food from the water and other things they get from the soil.

71

How Does Light Travel?

Can you tell what game the children in the picture are playing? Can the girl hear the boy as he looks for her? Why? Can she see him? Why?

The girl can hear the boy as he looks for her, but she cannot see him. Sound travels around corners, but light does not. Light travels only in straight lines.

How Light Travels

1. Get

| some clay | a hole puncher | three note cards | a flashlight | a book |

2. Stack the three cards. Punch a hole that goes through the middle of all the cards.

3. Make three small balls of clay. Stand one card in each clay ball.

4. Shine the light through the first hole. Does the light go through all the holes? Why?

5. Move the second card out of line. Shine the light through the first hole again. Does the light go through all the holes? Why?

6. Write down what you saw in the first experiment. Write down what you saw in the second experiment.

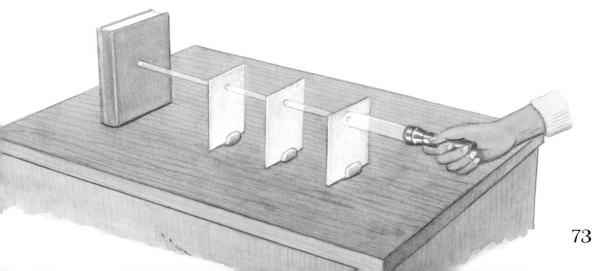

Some materials, such as wood and brick, do not let any light pass through them. They stop light. Can you see through those things at all? Frosted glass and waxed paper let only part of the light pass through. You cannot see clearly through them. Air, water, and clear glass let almost all of the light pass through them. You can see clearly through those things.

Shadows

How Are Shadows Made?

Shadows are made when objects stop light. Study the pictures. What things stop light? What things let only part of the light pass through? What things let almost all of the light pass through? What helped you decide?

Why Do Shadows Change Size and Move?

What happened to the shadows? Did they change size? Did they move? Why?

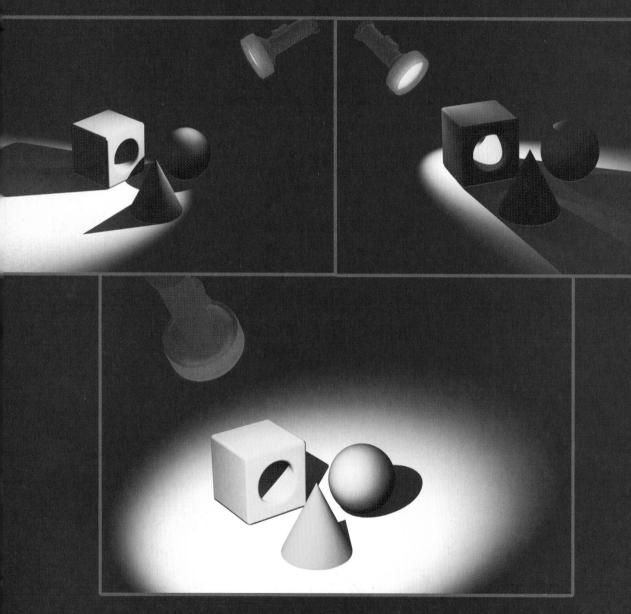

Shadows change size and move when the thing making the light moves.

What happened to the shadows? Did they change size? Did they move? Why?

Shadows change size and move when things making the shadows move.

"Every good gift and every perfect gift is from above, and cometh down from the Father of lights, with whom is no variableness, neither shadow of turning."

James 1:17

How Shadows Move and Change

1. Get

a ruler   some clay   a flashlight

2. Stand the ruler up in the clay.

3. Darken the room. Move the flashlight back and forth over the ruler. What happens to the shadow? Why?

4. Now hold the flashlight in one place and move the ruler back and forth under the light. What happens to the shadow of the ruler? Why?

5. Write down what you saw each time.

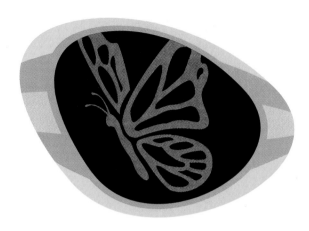

Living and Not Living

7

"Then king Darius wrote unto all people, . . . I make a decree, That in every dominion of my kingdom men tremble and fear before the God of Daniel: for he is the living God." Daniel 6:25-26

Look at the pictures. Which things are living? Which things are not living?

People are living things. Animals are living things.
Plants are living things.

How are living things alike?

Living Things Move

"And God created . . . every living creature that moveth."

Genesis 1:21

Many living things can move on their own. Animals are living things that move. Animals move in many ways. Some swim. Some fly. Others climb. Some animals hop and jump. Others walk and run. What other ways can animals move?

Some animals move in more than one way. A duck can swim, fly, and walk. A raccoon can walk, run, and climb. What other animals move in more than one way?

Some living things do not move from place to place on their own. Plants stay where they are unless something moves them to another place. Plants do move in a way. Some turn to face the sun. Some have leaves or flowers that fold up when it is dark or when they are touched. How do people move plants from place to place?

Living Things Have Needs

Living things need food. They need air and water.
Which picture shows someone taking air with him?
Which pictures show living things getting food or water?

"Behold the fowls of the air: for they sow not, neither do they reap, nor gather into barns; yet your heavenly Father feedeth them."　　　　　*Matthew 6:26*

Finding Out...

What Seeds Need to Grow

1. Get

some seeds

two paper towels

two small recloseable plastic bags

some water

some clear tape

2. Place some seeds on each paper towel.

3. Tape the seeds in place.

4. Place each towel in a plastic bag.

5. Add a half-inch of water to one bag.

6. Seal the bags.

7. Record what you did. Look at your seeds each day. Record what happens.

Living Things Respond

Living things respond to what is happening around them. Look at the pictures of the plant. How has it changed? Why has it changed?

Plants respond to changing light.

Animals respond to what is happening around them. How they respond is called *animal behavior*. Getting food and taking care of young are some animal behaviors.

Animals get food in many different ways. Some animals wait for ocean currents to bring it. Some store food for times when there isn't much food. Some animals travel to other places where they can find food. Some animals hunt, steal, trick, trap, or provide a service to get food. What ways of getting food are shown in these pictures?

Some baby animals get better care than others. Baby fish, lizards, and snakes do not get much care. They do not need much help to learn how to live. But baby birds, lions, tigers, monkeys, and bears get a lot of care. Mother cheetahs spend many hours teaching their young how to hunt. And monkeys spend a lot of time cleaning their young and teaching them how to behave.

Living Things Make New Living Things

The Bible says that living things bring forth after their kind. This means that apple trees produce apples. They will never make peaches or grapes. Dogs have puppies. They will never have kittens or lambs. It also means that living things make new living things.

Plants make new plants in different ways. Many plants make seeds. Then new plants grow from the seeds. Some plants make bulbs. Bulbs are tear-shaped stems, like onions. New plants grow from the bulbs. Sometimes a piece of a plant can grow into a new plant. Find the pictures of each way that plants make new plants.

Animals make baby animals in different ways. Many animals make eggs; then baby animals hatch from the eggs. Many animals make baby animals inside their bodies; then the baby animals are born. Find the pictures of each way.

Living Things Grow

All living things get bigger. They grow. Have you grown? Do plants grow? Do animals grow? How can you tell?

Some baby animals and plant seedlings grow up faster than others. Those animals that do not need much help learning how to live grow up quickly.

Some baby animals and plant seedlings look like their parents. When they are born, baby cows and baby giraffes look like their parents. But tadpoles have to change as they grow to look like their parents. Caterpillars change too.

Rabbits can leave their mothers six weeks after they are born. And within six months they can have babies of their own.

Plants and animals grow in different ways. Plants grow all their lives, but animals stop growing at some point. Also, plants grow new parts and animals do not. Plants keep making buds that grow into branches and leaves. But animals always have the same number of parts. Cats have four legs and one tail. They do not grow any more. What would happen if all living things grew in the same way?

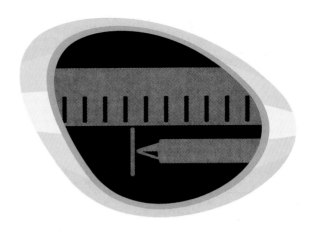

How Long
Is It?

8

"I lifted up mine eyes again, and looked, and behold a man with a measuring line in his hand. Then said I, Whither goest thou? And he said unto me, To measure Jerusalem, to see what is the breadth thereof, and what is the length thereof."

Zechariah 2:1-2

Is a cow heavier than a horse? Is a semi truck longer than a train car? Is a train faster than a boat? How much lemonade will a pitcher hold? How can you find out? You measure.

How Do You Measure?

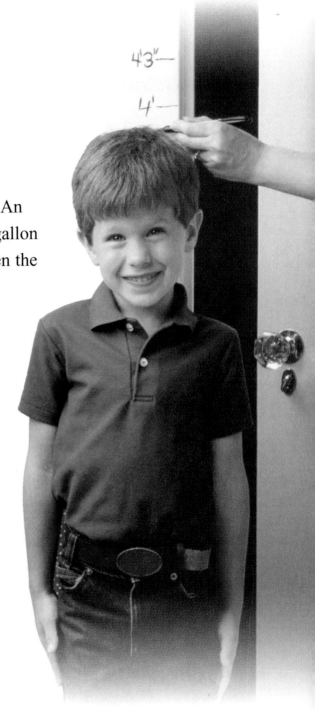

You use units to measure. An inch is a unit. So is a foot. A gallon and a pound are units too. Even the width of your finger can be a unit because a unit is an amount. How do people use units to measure?

When people measure, they compare a unit with something else to see how many units equal that thing.

In Bible times, one unit used for measuring was a span. A span is the length of the space between the tip of a man's thumb and the tip of his little finger.

Another unit used in Bible times was the cubit. A cubit is the length of the space from a man's elbow to the tip of his middle finger. Look at the man and his son measuring the same board. Will they get the same measurement? Why not?

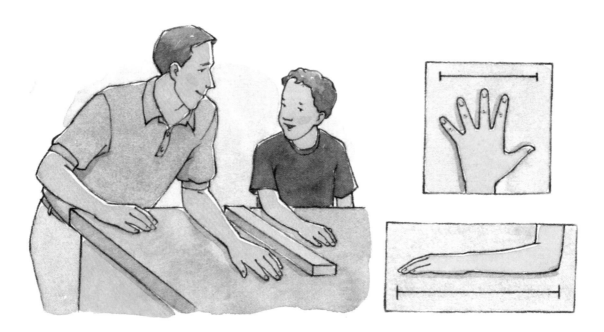

The father and his son would not get the same measurement because the father's arm is longer than the son's arm. What could they do to get the same measurement? They could use units that are the same. Units that are the same are called standard units.

You could make a standard unit by folding a piece of paper in half two times. The folds would make four spaces of the same size. Suppose you measured your book with your standard unit and found it to be five standard units long by three standard units wide. Would you ask the clerk at the bookstore for a book cover to fit a book five standard units long by three standard units wide? Why not?

You could not use your standard unit when talking to the clerk at the bookstore because she would not know your standard unit. If you want to tell people how long or wide something is, you should use a standard unit that they know.

Can you name some standard units that people know?

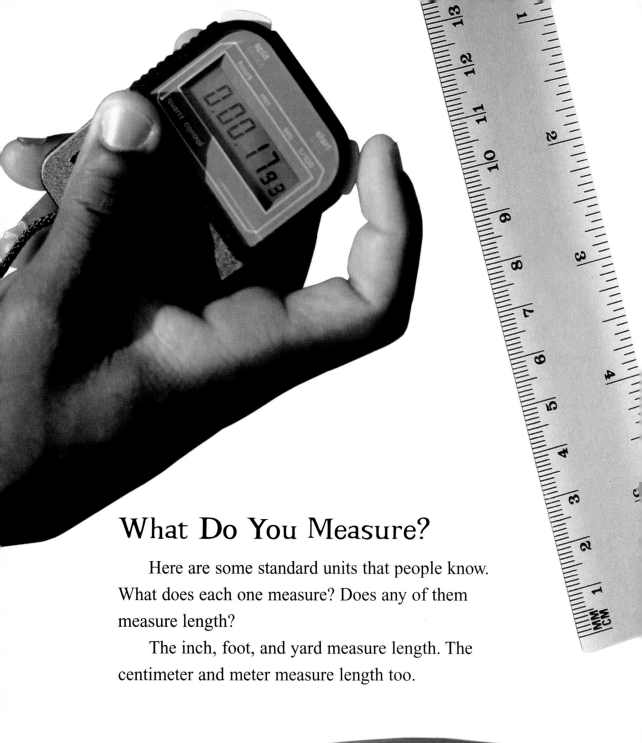

What Do You Measure?

Here are some standard units that people know. What does each one measure? Does any of them measure length?

The inch, foot, and yard measure length. The centimeter and meter measure length too.

Finding Out...

How to Measure Length

1. Get

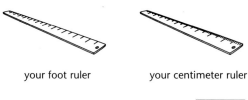

your foot ruler   your centimeter ruler

2. Get

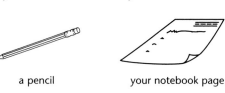

a pencil   your notebook page

3. Measure three objects in the room with your foot ruler.

4. Record the measurements on your notebook page.

5. Measure the same three objects in the room with your centimeter ruler.

6. Record the measurements on your notebook page.

Why Do You Measure?

Tell why the people are measuring length in these pictures.

A carpenter measures to make things fit together. An artist measures to make things fit into a certain space. A sports judge measures to see who wins.

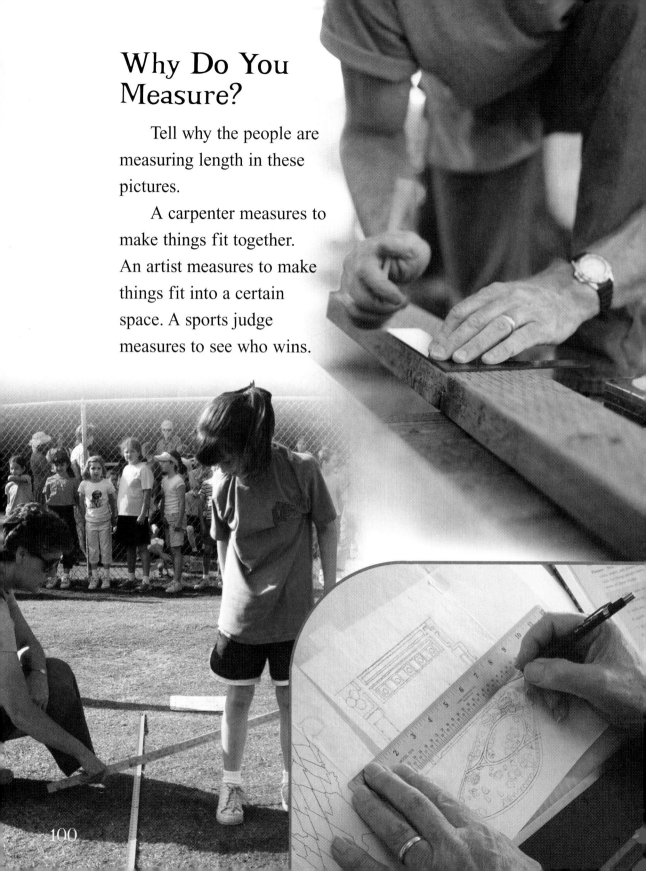

Why do scientists measure length? Sometimes scientists measure length to put things into groups. When they do that, they are classifying. Measuring length helps scientists classify rocks.

When scientists measure a rock, they measure across it at the biggest spot. They use a special tool called a caliper. Look at the picture of someone using a caliper on a rock. Can you see how it is used?

Classifying rocks by size results in five groups. Look at the chart of the groups.

Boulders	>10 inches across
Cobbles	2$^1/_2$ inches to 10 inches
Pebbles	$^1/_4$ inch to 2$^1/_2$ inches
Granules	$^1/_8$ inch to $^1/_4$ inch
Sand	< $^1/_8$ inch

How to Classify Rocks

1. Get

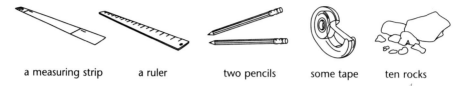

a measuring strip   a ruler   two pencils   some tape   ten rocks

2. Tape the measuring strip to your ruler.

3. Tape a pencil to the one-inch end of your ruler.

4. Lay a rock above the ruler on the desk. One side of the rock should touch the pencil.

5. Hold another pencil against the other side of the rock.

6. Look at the measuring strip. Record the type of each rock on your notebook page.

7. Display your rocks.

Sometimes scientists measure length to find out which group things belong to. When they do that, they are identifying. Measuring length helps scientists identify trees, butterflies, and prints.

When scientists measure a leaf, they measure its length from top to bottom. Ponderosa pines have needles five to eight inches long. Loblolly pines have needles six to nine inches long. And long-leaf pines have needles eight to eighteen inches long.

How Earth
Moves

9

Can you move but stay in one place? Yes, you jump and hop. Can you move from place to place? Yes, you can skip and run. You move in many different ways.

The earth moves in different ways too. But it does not hop or jump or skip. Do you know how it does move?

A Rotating Earth

The earth spins like a top. It goes around and around. It rotates. What other things rotate? Does a globe? Does a merry-go-round?

Because the earth rotates, there is a time of light and a time of darkness. The times of light and darkness happen over and over. Each cycle of light and darkness is called one day.

"And God called the light Day, and the darkness he called Night. And the evening and the morning were the first day."   *Genesis 1:5*

Finding Out... About Day and Night

1. Get

a globe   a flashlight   some plastic tack or a sticky note   your notebook   a pencil

2. Put some plastic tack or a sticky note on your state on the globe.

3. Turn off overhead lights. Shine the flashlight on the side of the globe with the marker.

4. Rotate the globe counterclockwise slowly. Is the marker always in the light?

5. Record what happened.

Because the earth rotates, the sun seems to move across the sky. The sun seems to move across the sky fourteen miles each minute. When the sun is right overhead, we say the clock time is noon. But the United States is so big that the states cannot all have the sun right overhead at the same time. So how do we decide when noon is in each state?

To make telling time easier, the whole earth is divided into twenty-four bands. They are called time zones. All the clocks in each band have the same time.

Look at the map. How many time zones are in
Canada? How many are in the United States? How many
are on this map?

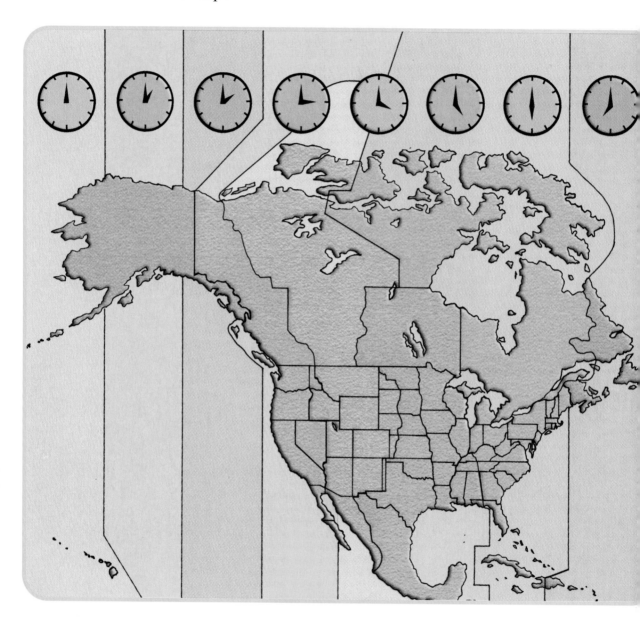

A Revolving Earth

The earth travels around the sun. It revolves. What other things revolve?

What happens because the earth revolves?

The earth always faces the sun at a little slant. Scientists call that slant "tilt." The weather changes because the earth revolves and because the earth is tilted.

"To every thing there is a season, and a time to every purpose under the heaven."   *Ecclesiastes 3:1*

Finding Out... About Seasons

1. Get

a globe   a flashlight   some plastic tack   your notebook   a pencil
or a sticky note

2. Put an *X* on the chalkboard. Put some plastic tack or a sticky note on your state. Hold the globe so that the North Pole faces the *X*.

3. Have a partner stand in the center of the room and shine the flashlight on the globe.

4. Walk around your partner. Keep the North Pole pointed at the *X*. Your partner should keep the light shining on the globe.

5. Record on your notebook page where the light shined on the globe.

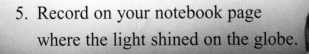

Each cycle of weather changes is called a year. The earth rotates 365 and one-fourth times in a year. But when you look at a calendar, you usually see only 365 days. What happened to the extra one-fourth day? We don't count it until there are four. Then every fourth year, one whole day is added to the calendar in the month of February. This fourth year is called leap year. Look at this year's calendar. Does February have twenty-nine days? If so, this is a leap year.

Spring

Summer

Fall

Winter

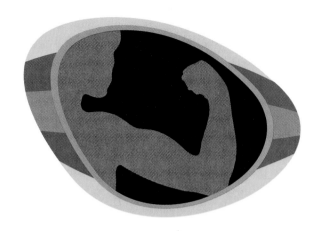

Your Muscles

10

Has anyone ever said to you, "Make a muscle?" What did you do? You probably made a fist and bent your arm. Then your "muscle" came up as a hump on your upper arm. But that is only one of the many muscles God put in your body.

Names of Muscles

Each muscle has a name. The name may be a long, hard word, but it tells something about the muscle. For example, the name *pectoralis major* tells the place and size of the muscle. *Pectoralis* means "chest area" and *major* means "large." The name *deltoid* tells the shape of the muscle. It means "triangular."

Structure of Muscles

Muscles are made of long, thin threads. Each thread is called a fiber. Have you ever seen the fibers in chicken muscle? They look like the strands of fiber in a rope.

About Muscle Fibers

1. Get

a short, thin piece of raw steak or chicken   a darning needle   two microscope slides   red and blue food coloring

rubbing alcohol   a small bottle   a tablespoon   a magnifying glass

2. Put one drop of red and one drop of blue food coloring in a tablespoon. Fill up the rest of the spoon with rubbing alcohol. Store in the bottle.

3. Put the piece of meat on a microscope slide. Pick the muscle fiber apart with a darning needle. Put several drops of stain on the meat. Put a second slide on as a cover.

4. Look at the muscle with a magnifying glass. In your notebook, sketch what the fibers look like.

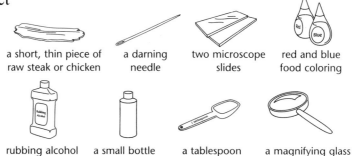

Kinds of Muscles

You have three kinds of muscles. Each kind looks different, is found in a different place, and has a different job. *Skeletal muscles* are striped or grooved like a plowed field. Can you guess where they are found? Can you tell from the name what their job might be?

Smooth muscles are another kind of muscle. They are called smooth because they do not have any light and dark stripes. The stomach, intestines, blood vessels, and bladder have smooth muscles. Round places, like the opening of your eye and your throat, also have smooth muscles. Can you guess the job of smooth muscles?

Cardiac muscles are found only in the heart. *Cardiac* comes from a word meaning "heart." Cardiac muscles are striped, but not as clearly or roughly as the skeletal muscles. What do the cardiac muscles do?

Look at the microscope pictures of the muscles. Can you find the picture of each kind of muscle?

Jobs of Muscles

As you may have already guessed, skeletal muscles move your bones. But they move other body parts too, like your eyes and tongue. Most of the time skeletal muscles work in pairs.

One muscle in a pair will tighten and pull a bone in one direction. Then it relaxes, and the other muscle in the pair will tighten and pull the bone in the other direction.

Look at the drawings of muscle pairs in action. Which muscle in the pair is doing the action?

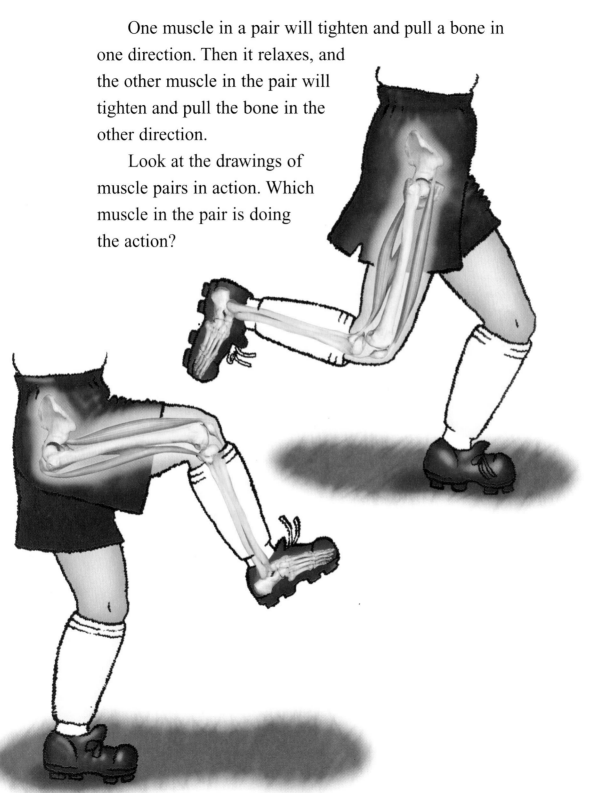

The smooth muscles are in charge of moving things such as food in the body. Use one finger to follow the path of the food on the drawing of the digestive system. Can you see how the muscles keep the food moving along?

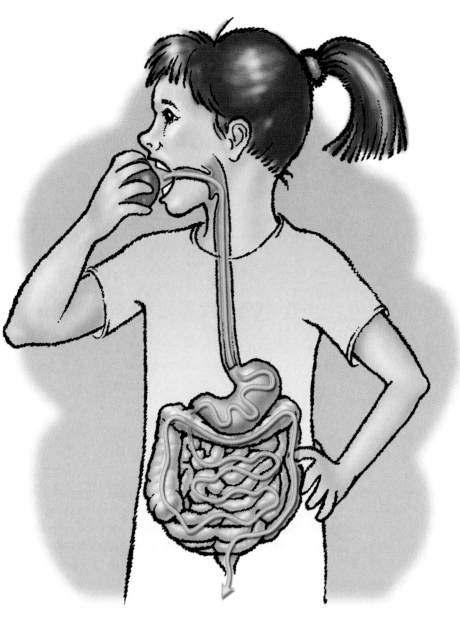

The cardiac muscles move blood through the heart. They pump blood out into the long hollow tubes called *blood vessels*. This system of the heart and blood vessels is called the *circulatory system*. How is it a little bit like a circle?

 **About Heart Rate**

1. Get

a stopwatch   your notebook

2. Have your teacher find your heart rate. Record this number on your notebook page.

3. Have a partner time you while you run in place for thirty seconds. Let your teacher find your heart rate again. Record this number on your notebook page.

4. Fill in the bar graph on your notebook page. Did your heart rate go up or down? Why?

"For bodily exercise profiteth little: but godliness is profitable unto all things, having promise of the life that now is, and of that which is to come."
I Timothy 4:8

124

Layers of
the Earth

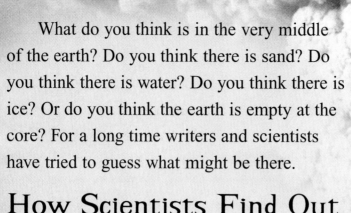

11

What do you think is in the very middle of the earth? Do you think there is sand? Do you think there is water? Do you think there is ice? Or do you think the earth is empty at the core? For a long time writers and scientists have tried to guess what might be there.

One writer named Jules Verne made up a whole book about some people going to the middle of the earth. But that is only a story. Scientists want to know the facts.

How Scientists Find Out About the Earth's Inside

It is not hard to find out about the outside of things. Let's say you get a birthday present. You know it's a birthday present because it's in birthday wrapping paper. You know something about its size just by looking at it. In one way, the earth is like a birthday present. Scientists can find out quite a lot about the outside part because they can see it.

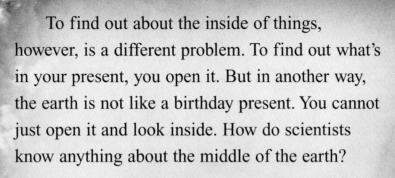

To find out about the inside of things, however, is a different problem. To find out what's in your present, you open it. But in another way, the earth is not like a birthday present. You cannot just open it and look inside. How do scientists know anything about the middle of the earth?

Signs from Inside

Most of what scientists know about the inside of the earth they learn from earthquakes and volcanoes.

When there is an earthquake, scientists measure how much and how long the ground shakes. What they record helps them tell what kind of rock is under the surface.

Sometimes volcanoes throw out melted rock called *lava*. This rock comes from much farther down in the earth than man has ever been able to dig. What can scientists learn about the inside of the earth from lava?

Men drill holes in the earth and pull out samples of rock. Have you ever put a straw into a drink and closed off the top of the straw with your finger? What happened when you lifted the straw up? Some of the drink stayed in the straw, didn't it? Something very much the same happens when scientists drill into the earth for rock samples. Then they study the sample and record the kind of material it is, what layers it is in, and how deep in the earth it was.

Sometimes men go under the ocean to drill holes in the earth. Why do you think they go to the ocean floor to drill?

A long time ago, many people tried to find underground water by cutting forked tree branches and walking around with them pointed down. These branches are called "divining rods." Divining rods were supposed to shake when they were carried over ground that had water under it. Do you think underground water would make a branch shake?

Oil men sometimes try to find oil underground with magnets and machines that vibrate. These ways of trying to find out what is underground are called "doodlebugging." "Doodle" means "fool." What do you think the name tells about divining rods and other gadgets like it?

What Scientists Find Out About the Earth's Inside

Layers of the Earth

Scientists think the earth is made of three layers. The top layer of the earth is mostly solid rock called the crust. How thick is the crust? If the earth were an apple, the crust would be as thin as the apple's skin. The crust is about 2 to 4 miles thick under the oceans. Under some mountains, the crust can be up to 44 miles deep.

Under the crust is the layer of earth called the mantle. It is about 1,800 miles thick. If we again compare the earth to an apple, the mantle would be as thick as the white part under the skin of the apple. Geologists believe the earth's mantle is as hot as 3,000 degrees Fahrenheit.

Deep in the center of the earth is the third layer called the core. If we compare the earth to an apple once again, the earth's core is as thick as the center, or core, of the apple. The earth's core is about 4,200 miles from one side to the other. Temperatures there are probably as high as 7,200 degrees Fahrenheit.

About the Earth's Layers

1. Get

some clay from your
teacher (You need
three colors.)

a piece of
thread

2. Build a small "earth." Make a small ball of one color of clay. Put a layer of another color around that. Next put a thin layer of the last color around.

3. Holding the thread tightly between both hands, slice through the clay to the center. Take the thread out. Make another slice at a slant so that part of the "earth" can be lifted out like a piece of cake.

4. Draw what you see. Name the layers of your "earth."

Materials of Each Part

The surface of the crust is covered by oceans and land. Do you know the name of an ocean? Have you ever seen an ocean? How did it look? Oceans cover more of the earth than dry land does.

The land at the top of the crust is divided by the oceans. The big parts are called *continents*. Smaller parts are called *islands*. Continents and islands are made up of rocks and soil.

Do you remember where fossils are found? Do you think there are any fossils in the mantle or the core? Why not?

The mantle is probably made of a rock called *iron magnesium*. This rock is a mixture of a heavy metal and a lighter one that can burn brightly.

Scientists think that the outer part of the core is melted iron and nickel. Nickel is a silver-colored metal that can be made magnetic. The very center of the core is most likely almost solid iron.

Can you imagine how heavy the earth must be?

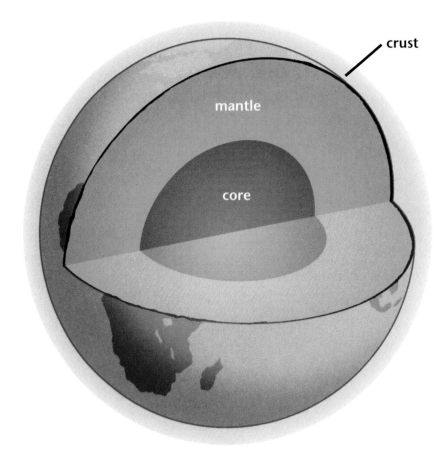

"In the beginning God created the heaven and the earth. And the earth was without form, and void; and darkness was upon the face of the deep."   *Genesis 1:1-2*

Where Things Live

CHAPTER TWELVE

"The foxes have holes, and the birds of the air have nests."   *Matthew 8:20*

Kinds of Homes

God made every living thing to live in a particular place. He made each living thing able to get what it needs from that place.

Habitats

Name some places where animals live. Have you seen some wild animal homes? The place where an animal or plant lives is a *habitat*. Three habitats for animals are water, air, and soil. Can you think of animals that live in each of these places? Most animals live in one of these places.

Some animals live on or in other living things. A tick lives on another animal, often a dog. The skin of a dog can be a tick's habitat. A tapeworm lives inside another animal. Its habitat may be the stomach of that animal.

Environment

Everything that is around an organism in a habitat is called the *environment*. The word comes from two words that mean "to put in a circle." Look at the picture of the raccoons. What is their environment?

> A habitat has what the organism, the living thing, needs to live. It has the right temperature, the right food, and the right amount of light or darkness.

Biomes

Many plants and animals can share the same place. A large area that takes in all the plants and animals in the same environment is a *biome*. Some biomes are on land, and others are in the water.

Two land biomes are a desert and a forest of evergreen trees. Would a polar bear live in a desert? Would a cactus grow in an evergreen forest? Why are the bear and the cactus out of place in these pictures?

One water biome is a lake. What living things would have a habitat there?

Parts of an Environment

Scientists study how everything in a habitat acts together. They call this study *ecology*. That word means "the study of the home."

Parts that Are not Living

The sun is important to most environments. How brightly the sun shines and how long it shines will determine what plants can live in a place. The sun also can cause the animals to stay or leave. If a place got too hot, the animals might go somewhere else. What would happen to the plants?

Soil is another part of the environment. Not all soils are alike. Some soil will grow only certain kinds of plants. Those plants can then be food for only certain kinds of animals.

Let's say that a place has the kind of sunlight and soil that grows only grass. Animals that live mostly on grass could live there. But could animals that eat fruits live there? Why not?

Wind can also help determine which plants and animals live in a place. Many organisms cannot stand hard winds all the time. Along ocean coasts the wind blows nearly all the time. Seagulls do well on ocean coasts. They sail along on the wind. But how do you think a small wren would do?

Only certain plants can live in wind. Look at this picture. How have these trees grown because of the wind in their environment? Which way does the wind always blow there?

How does wind change the environment of water biomes? Have you ever seen waves tossed by wind? High waves will make life harder for some organisms and easier for others.

Finding Out... About Wind

1. Get

    the foot of an old   a wire hanger   some glue
        stocking

2. Make a "wind sock" the way your teacher shows you.

3. Take the windsock outside. Hold it up to catch any wind. Is the breeze blowing gently? Is there a strong wind? Which way is it blowing?

4. Record what the windsock looked like when you held it up outside. Tell which way the wind blew.

The most important part of an environment is water. How much rain falls and when it falls make a place a desert or a thick jungle. Jungles get more rain than deserts.

Some environments are all water. Is a pond all water? How about a river?

What happens to a swamp when there is no rain? Does it become some other kind of environment? What will happen to the plants and animals?

Do you help water your garden or lawn? Why do you water it?

Parts That Are Living

All living things in an area make a community. We can see most of the living things in an environment. But a few living things are too small to see.

Name all the living things you can see in the picture.

Choose one kind of flower in the picture. How many flowers of that kind are there in the picture? You have just found one plant population.

All living things of one kind in an area make up a *population*. All plants of one kind are called a plant population. All animals of one kind make up an animal population.

How many different plant populations are shown in the picture?

When you count how many of one kind of animal or plant live in an area, you do a population count. How would you like to do a population count here?

"Are not five sparrows sold for two farthings, and not one of them is forgotten before God?"   Luke 12:6

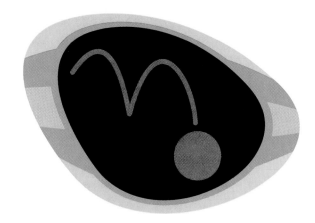

Motion

"And the Egyptians were urgent upon the people, that they might send them out of the land in haste."

What is happening in these pictures that is alike?

Everything is moving.
How is everything moving?
Why is everything moving?

How Things Move

Scientists use both words and numbers to describe. If they describe a tree, they describe its size with numbers and its color with words. If they describe a car, they describe its speed with numbers and its shape with words. If they describe motion, they use both words and numbers too.

What do they describe about motion using numbers? They describe how far things move by using numbers. They measure distance. They describe how fast things move by using numbers. They measure speed.

About Speed and Distance

1. Get

a stopwatch or a watch
with a second hand

two small
model cars

a tape measure

2. Have a partner gently push one of the cars when you say "Go." Start your watch at the same time. When the car stops on its own, stop the watch or call out the time. How many seconds did the car move?

3. Measure how far the car moved.

4. Leave the first car where it stopped. Push the other car harder. Time and measure its travel. How far did the second car go? For how long did it move?

5. Record what happened.

What do you describe about motion by using words? You describe the way things move by using words. You describe how they look to you.

Pretend you are in a moving car and you see a man standing in a field. Would he look as if he were moving? Pretend you are standing in the field and you see a man driving by in a car. Would the man in the car look as if he were moving? Sometimes the way moving things look depends on where you are.

Why Things Move

Sir Isaac Newton, a scientist from long ago, was interested in motion. He came up with some ideas that describe why things move. He tested and proved his ideas. People today often call his ideas *Newton's laws of motion.*

The first law of motion says that an object keeps doing what it is doing until some force causes a change. A book stays at rest until you lift it. A marble stays at rest until you hit it with another marble. Look at the pictures. Name other examples of this law.

If you are in a car that stops quickly, your body keeps moving forward after the car has stopped. Seatbelts stop you from moving too far forward, but you still move.

First Law: An object keeps doing what it is doing until some force causes a change.

The second law says that it is easier to change the speed and direction of a light thing than a heavy thing. Using the same amount of force, you can throw a baseball faster than you can throw a basketball. You can more easily change the direction of a badminton birdie than the direction of a softball.

The second law also says that the more force you use, the faster a thing will change its speed or direction. The harder you pedal your bike, the faster you will change your speed. The harder you throw a basketball, the faster you will change its direction.

A racing car is an example of both parts of the second law of motion. A racing car has a very light body, so it is easy to change its speed and direction. A racing car has a powerful engine. A very powerful engine has more force to make the speed or direction change faster.

Second Law: It is easier to change the speed or direction of a light thing than a heavy thing. And the more force you use, the faster a thing will change its speed or direction.

The third law says that for every action there is an equal and opposite reaction. That means that when something starts moving, something else moves in the opposite direction. A balloon pushes air out one way. That is an action. The reaction is the crazy zipping of the balloon through the air in the other direction. Can you tell the action and reaction in this example?

Third Law: For every action there is an equal and opposite reaction.

Tell the actions and reactions
shown in these pictures.

159

Finding Out... About the Laws of Motion

1. Get

a stopwatch or a watch
with a second hand

two small model cars

a tape measure

2. Put one car one foot in front of you. Push the other car so that it bumps the first car. Time how long the first car moves.

3. Write down what happened when the cars bumped. Use both words and numbers.

Ocean
Shorelines

CHAPTER FOURTEEN

Have you ever seen an ocean? An ocean is a huge body of water. You cannot see all of it at once. You can see only a little bit of it as you stand on the shore. The ocean is a world of its own, with underwater mountains and valleys and sea plants and sea animals. Since we cannot study the whole ocean at once, let's look at just the shoreline. The shoreline is where the great ocean meets the land.

There are many different kinds of shorelines. Large stones and boulders form *rocky shorelines*.

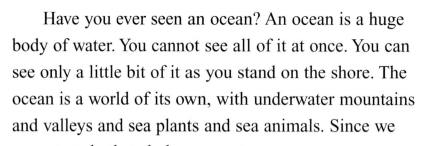

b

rocky

marsh

Most *beaches* are sandy. A few are muddy, and a few are covered with pebbles and stones.

Some shores are low, wet edges called *marshes*. They are usually grassy.

Bluffs are high ridges of land or rock along the shore.

sandy

Sometimes shorelines change. Storms or waves may move sand and mud or wear away land and rock.

Men can change shorelines also. They change the shape of a natural shore or dig out a new harbor. A *harbor* is water that is sheltered by land and is deep enough for ships to float in.

Hundreds of years ago sailors found many good harbors along the East Coast of our country. Big cities usually grow up around good harbors. Why do you think that happens?

Beaches

More people know about sandy beaches than about any other kind of shoreline. They like to go there to enjoy the water and the sunshine, to walk along the surf, to play, and to rest. Have you ever been to a beach? What did it look like?

Not all beaches look alike. What makes these beaches look different from each other?

What Is in Sand?

Parts of Sand

What is that grainy material on beaches that sticks to your wet feet? On some beaches it is mostly tiny bits of shell. How do you think shells get broken into such small pieces?

Most sand contains *quartz*. Quartz is a hard, crystal-like material. Look at the close-up picture of sand. Can you see the bits of quartz?

Some sand also has black material in it. The black parts are *basalt,* part of lava rock. Did you know before that there are black beaches? Where do you think such beaches are?

Size of Sand

Some sand has very tiny grains. Some has large grains. Scientists measure the size of sand grains by shaking them through a wire screen. All grains smaller than one-twelfth of an inch fall through. What falls through is called sand.

A Bird on the Sand

This bird lives on seashores. It is small, with long legs and a long pointed beak. It is the sandpiper.

It eats worms, insects, and shrimp. How do you think it gets this food out of the sand?

The sandpiper runs behind the waves that roll back to the sea, looking for food washed up by the water. As it goes it makes a merry piping sound, from which it gets its name.

167

Finding Out... About Sand

1. Get

construction paper   a toothpick   a pencil   a magnifying glass   some sand   your notebook page

2. Pour a few grains of sand on a piece of construction paper. Look at it under the magnifying glass. Use the toothpick to move the grains around. Can you tell which grains are parts of shell, which are quartz, and which are basalt?

3. Record what you see.

"How precious also are thy thoughts unto me, O God! how great is the sum of them! If I should count them, they are more in number than the sand."

Psalm 139:17-18

Living by the Shore

People who live on the coasts often try to keep the sand from washing away. They build *breakwaters*.

How do you think breaking up the water helps keep the shore from being worn away?

Some houses along shores are built on stilts. Why do you think the houses are built like that?

"*Fear ye not me? saith the Lord: will ye not tremble at my presence, which have placed the sand for the bound of the sea by a perpetual decree, that it cannot pass it: and though the waves thereof toss themselves, yet can they not prevail; though they roar, yet can they not pass over it?*"

Jeremiah 5:22

Little Things Count

Our great God created a beautiful world. In this world He put many resources, or things that we can use. God expects us to use those resources wisely. One way that we can use them wisely is to recycle.

Recycling helps to keep things that we have used from just being thrown away. Old things can be turned into new things. This helps us to save some of our resources.

How can we recycle? In some areas, items to be recycled must be taken to a recycling center. This place has many boxes. Items must be separated and put into their proper boxes. Then they can be recycled.

In other places, items at home are put into a special box called a recycling bin. This box is placed at the street next to the trash can. Workers in a recycling truck pick up the items.

What can we recycle? Newspaper is one of the things that we can recycle. We can also recycle glass and cardboard. We help take care of God's earth by recycling. Even little things can make a big difference!

Useful Terms

amber Fossilized tree sap that looks like light yellow stone. Insects are often found trapped in amber.

annual A plant that grows and lives for one year.

artery A blood vessel that carries blood away from the heart to other parts of the body.

astronauts People who travel in space.

attract To draw toward oneself.

basalt A hard, dark, glassy rock formed from cooled lava.

biennial A plant that lives for only two years.

biome A major region of life, known by its plant life and climate, such as a desert or a forest.

blood vessel A tube in the body through which blood is pumped. Arteries and veins are blood vessels.

bluff A steep hill or cliff along a shore or riverbank.

cardiac muscles The muscles of the heart.

cartilage Tough, flexible tissue, usually found between bones, that absorbs shock and eases movement in joints.

circulatory system The system of the heart and blood vessels that transports blood throughout the body.

community A group of living things that live in the same area.

continent A large mass of land, larger than an island. There are seven continents on Earth: North America, South America, Europe, Africa, Asia, Australia, and Antarctica.

core The center or most important part of something. The molten center of the earth.

creation The work of God in making the universe.

crust The top layer. The earth's crust is made of oceans, continents, and islands.

deciduous trees Trees that have a winter period of dormancy.

ecology A study of how everything in a habitat acts together.

environment Everything that surrounds an organism.

equator An imaginary line around the center of the earth, halfway between the north and south poles.

evolution The theory that the universe made itself.

fitness Good physical condition.

force A push or pull.

fossil Natural evidence of a long-dead plant or animal, whether an imprint in rock, a petrified bone, or some other sign.

friction Resistance caused by rubbing. A force that slows or stops the motion of two things touching each other.

garden A plot of land for growing plants.

gardener A person who takes care of a garden.

globe A spherical (ball-shaped) map of Earth or another planet.

gravity The force that draws objects together; the force that gives people weight and keeps people and objects on the earth from flying off into space.

habitat A place where an animal is found naturally; a living environment.

hinge joint A joint that moves like a hinge. The knee and elbow are hinge joints.

involuntary Occurring without thought or conscious command; not able to be controlled by the will.

iron A metal that is attracted by magnets and is used in making steel.

joint The place where two or more bones come together and move against each other. The knee and the elbow are both joints.

lava Melted rock.

living The state of being alive. Living things react to the world around them and make other living things like themselves. They need food, water, and air.

magnesium A light, hard metal that burns brightly.

magnetic force The force that attracts metal to a magnet.

mantle The layer of the earth under the crust.

marshes Low, wet, grassy areas along the shoreline.

mechanical force A force that stops and starts movement.

missionary A person who travels around the world telling mankind about God.

model A small copy of an object.

mulch Material that is put around plants to keep roots safe.

muscle Tissue composed of fibers that tighten or relax to move the parts of the body.

nursery A place that grows and sells small plants.

observing Watching.

ocean A large body of water between continents. Earth's surface is approximately three-fourths ocean.

opaque Not capable of letting light through.

organism A living plant or animal.

perennial A plant that will grow and bloom for many years.

pivot joint A joint in which one bone rotates around another one.

population All the organisms of the same kind that live in a particular area.

pruning Cutting off parts of a plant in order to allow the remaining parts to grow better.

reflect To bounce back light or sound from a surface.

reflection A sound or image that is reflected.

repel To push away.

revolving Moving in orbit around an object. Earth revolves around the sun.

rotation Spinning. Earth rotates on its axis.

shadow A dark area where an object is blocking the light.

skeleton The framework of bones and cartilage that gives the body shape and support and helps it move.

standard measurement The measurement that is used as a basis of all other measurement.

tide The regular change in the level of the oceans that is caused by the moon's gravitational pull.

translucent Allowing light but not clear images through.

transplant To dig up a plant and move it to a new location.

vein A blood vessel that carries blood to the heart.

vertebrae The bones of the spinal column; backbones.

voluntary Occurring according to the will or on conscious command.

Index

basalt 166

beach 163

biome 138

bluff 163

bones 45-48

caliper 101

community 145

continents 133

core 131

creation 15

crust 130

doodlebugging 129

ecology 139

environment 137

evolution 15

force 30

fossil 16-26

friction 39-42

garden 4

gardener 2

gravity 30-32

habitat 136

harbor 164

islands 133

joints 50-51

lava 127

light 68-74

magnet 34-36

mantle 130

marsh 163

muscle 116

Newton, Sir Isaac 154

population 146

population count 148

quartz 166

revolve 111

rotate 106

sandpiper 167

shadow 75

skeleton 44, 52

Illustration Credits

John Bjerk 110, 134
Matthew Bjerk 4, 8 (top right), 22 (top), 38 (bottom right), 44, 58, 66, 75-77, 82, 104, 112, 114, 141, 162, 169
James Hargis 5-6, 22-23, 28, 59, 73 (bottom), 110, 130-31, 134
Brian Johnson 28
Deborah King 9 (top), 21 (top), 36 (top), 42 (top), 46 (top), 49 (top), 61 (top), 73 (top), 78 (top), 85 (top), 99 (top), 102 (top), 108 (top), 113 (top), 118 (top), 124 (top), 132 (top), 142 (top), 152 (top), 160 (top), 168 (top)
Duane Nichols 8 (bottom)
David Schuppert 26
Lynda Slattery 10-12, 47, 172-73

The following artists are represented by Wilkinson Studios, LLC:
Linda Bittner 94, 138, 167
Robin Brickman 3
Phyllis Pollema Cahill 70, 96
Donna Catanese 92, 129
Mike Dammer 56, 64-65, 109, 153
Bob Masheris 63, 106
Wendy Rasmussen 89, 139
Kate Sweeney 48, 50-52, 117, 120-23
Bobbi Tull 146-47
Nicole Wong 72, 97

Photo Credits

The following agencies and individuals have furnished materials to meet the photographic needs of this textbook. We wish to express our gratitude to them for their important contribution.

Able Stock
Suzanne Altizer
Artemis Images
John Bjerk
Corbis
COREL Corporation
Digital Vision
J.A. Franklin
Dr. Kenneth Frederick
Freedonia Seeds
Getty Images

Toef Hadar
Brenda Hansen
Edwin G. Huffman
Breck Kent
Joyce Landis
Peter LaTourette
Miriam Mitchem
Greg Moss
National Park Service
Susan Perry
Dr. Margene Ranieri

Six Flags Over Georgia
The South Carolina Aquarium
Transparencies, Inc.
University of Idaho Forest Research Nursery
Unusual Films
Ward's Natural Science Establishment
World Bank

Cover
Ryan McVay/Getty Images (tiger); PhotoLink/Getty Images (background)

Front Matter
Unusual Films iii, iv (marble), v (marble); Robert Glusic/Getty Images iv (windmill); Jess Alford/Getty Images iv (cheetahs); PhotoLink/Getty Images v (arm); Corbis v (planes); Pat Powers and Cherryl Schafer/Getty Images v (flower); Susan Perry v (fossil)

Chapter 1
Ryan McVay/Getty Images 2; PhotoLink/Getty Images 5, 7 (top left); John A. Rizzo/Getty Images 7 (bottom right); Kenneth Frederick 7 (background); courtesy of Freedonia Seeds 8; Susan Perry 9

Chapter 2
National Park Service 14; C. Borland/PhotoLink/Getty Images 15; BJU Press Files 16 (left); Jeremy Woodhouse/Getty Images 16 (right); S. Meltzer/PhotoLink/Getty Images 16-17 (bottom); Siede Preis/Getty Images 17 (top); Jack Hollingsworth/Getty Images 17 (bottom right); PhotoLink/Getty Images 17 (bottom left, background); Unusual Films 18, 21; Susan Perry 19 (top left, bottom left), 24, 25 (all); Ward's Natural Science Establishment 19 (right), 20; Russell Illig/Getty Images 27

Chapter 3

Karl Weatherly/Getty Images 30; Joaquin Palting/Getty Images 30-1 (top); Nicola Sutton/Life File/Getty Images 31 (inset); StockTrek/Getty Images 31 (bottom left); Russell Illig/Getty Images 32-33; PhotoLink/Getty Images 33 (top right), 37 (left), 39 (top right), 41 (left); John Bjerk 33 (bottom right); Unusual Films 34, 35 (both), 36, 40, 42 (all); Robert Glusic/Getty Images 37 (right); Lawrence M. Sawyer/Getty Images 38 (left); Geostock/Getty Images 38 (inset); Alex L. Fradkin/Getty Images 39 (top left); Arthur S. Aubry/Getty Images 39 (bottom right); Susan Perry 39 (bottom left); Glen Allison/Getty Images 39 (bottom middle); David Buffington/Getty Images 41 (top right); Corbis 41 (bottom right)

Chapter 4

Unusual Films 44 (both), 45 (both), 46; Joyce Landis 49; PhotoLink/Getty Images 52, 53 (top right, bottom); Karl Weatherly/Getty Images 53 (top left); Corbis 54

Chapter 5

C Square Studios/Getty Images 57 (all); Edwin G. Huffman/World Bank 60 (left); Toef Hadar/World Bank 60 (others); Unusual Films 61; Doug Menuez/Getty Images 62

Chapter 6

PhotoLink/Getty Images 68, 68-69 (bottom inset), 69 (middle), 71 (left), 75 (left); Andrew Ward/Life File/Getty Images 69; R. Morley/PhotoLink/Getty Images 69 (bottom); Daisuke Morita/Getty Images 71 (right); Unusual Films 74 (left, right), 78; Susan Perry 74 (background); Doug Menuez/Getty Images 75 (right); Jack Hollingsworth/Getty Images 75 (background)

Chapter 7

C Squared Studio/Getty Images 80 (violin), 80-81 (crayons, popsicle); G.K. and Vikki Hart/Getty Images 80 (dog); PhotoLink/Getty Images 81 (rose, family); Geostock/Getty Images 81 (boy); Corbis 82 (top left), 84 (top right, bottom right), 87 (left); Alan and Sandy Carey/Getty Images 82 (inset); Geostock/Getty Images 82 (bottom); Nancy R. Cohen/Getty Images 83 (left); Joyce Landis 83 (all others); PhotoLink/Getty Images 84 (left); Unusual Films 85 (all); Russell Illig/Getty Images 86 (background); Suzanne Altizer 86 (insets); Breck Kent 87 (right), 88 (top left); Karl Weatherly/Getty Images 88 (top right); PhotoLink/Getty Images 88 (bottom); Jess Alford/Getty Images 90 (top); Geostock/Getty Images 90 (bottom left), J. A. Franklin 90 (bottom right); Pat Powers and Cherryl Schafer/Getty Images 91 (bottom right); Miriam Mitchem 91 (others)

Chapter 8

PhotoLink/Getty Images 95, 98 (top left); Susan Perry 98 (top right), 100 (bottom right); Spike Mafford/Getty Images 98 (bottom); Unusual Films 99, 101, 102 (both), 103, (both); Greg Moss 100 (bottom left); Ryan McVay/Getty Images 100 (top right); University of Idaho Forest Research Nursery 104

Chapter 9

R. Morley/PhotoLink/Getty Images 107 (left); PhotoLink/Getty Images 107 (right), 111 (top, bottom), 114 (background); Unusual Films 108, 113; Courtesy of Six Flags Over Georgia 111; Corbis 114 (top, middle, bottom)

Chapter 10

Unusual Films 116, 118; PhotoLink/Getty Images 119 (top); Dr. Margene Ranieri 119 (insets); Susan Perry 124

Chapter 11

C. Sherburne/PhotoLink/Getty Images 126-27 (background); PhotoLink/Getty Images 126 (left), 127 (inset); S. Alden/PhotoLink/Getty Images 126 (inset); Geostock/Getty Images 128 (left); Kim Steele/Getty Images 128 (right); Unusual Films 128 (foreground), 132; Jeremy Hoare/Life File/Getty Images 133

Chapter 12

Breck Kent 136, 137, 141; PhotoLink/Getty Images 140 (both), 144 (left); Susan Perry 142; Bruce Heineman/Getty Images 143 (top); Adalberto Rios Szalay/Sexto Sol/Getty Images 143 (bottom); Digital Vision 144 (right); Geostock/Getty Images 144 (bottom); Frank and Joyce Burek/Getty Images 145 (turtle); Courtesy: the South Carolina Aquarium 145 (others); Jeremy Woodhouse/Getty Images 148

Chapter 13

Corbis 150 (top); Doug Menuez/ Getty Images 150 (bottom); COREL Corporation 151; Unusual Films 152, 160; Brenda Hansen 154 (top); Unusual Films Courtesy of Six Flags Over Georgia 154 (bottom); Rim Light/PhotoLink/Getty Images 155 (both), Rim Light/Getty Images 156 (bottom); PhotoLink/Getty Images 156 (right); C Indianapolis Motor Speedway (http://www.artemisimages.com) 157; Lawrence M. Sawyer/Getty Images 158; Corbis 159 (left); PhotoLink/Getty Images 159 (background, bottom right); Karl Weatherly/Getty Images 159 (top right)

Chapter 14

John Wang/Getty Images 162 (both), 165 (left); AbleStock 163 (top); Edmond Van Hoorick/Getty Images 163 (bottom); C. Borland/PhotoLink/Getty Images 164; PhotoLink/Getty Images 165 (right); Unusual Films 166, 168; Peter LaTourette 167; Jane Faircloth/Transparencies, Inc. 169; S. Alden/PhotoLink/Getty Images 170

Back Matter

John Wang/Getty Images 174; PhotoLink/Getty Images 175, 177; Steve Cole/Getty Images 176; S. Meltzer/PhotoLink/Getty Images 178; Nancy R. Cohen/Getty Images 179; Unusual Films 184

Science 1 Start your student on the path of scientific inquiry with an introduction to the senses, heat, sound, animals, and heavenly bodies—presenting God as Creator of all things.

Science 2 Present God's earth and His creation clearly as your student studies bones, plants, the shape and movement of the earth, natural forces, and shorelines.

Science 3 Direct your student's natural curiosity by helping him describe what God has created. Through studies of classification of animals, the solar system, skin, photosynthesis, birds, mass, and weight, your student will increase his knowledge of the world God made.

$5 + 2$

Grace